C000003223

Meditation

*Self Development Guide For Peace, Mindfulness and
Kundalini Awakening and Expand Your Subconscious
Mind Power To Beat Anxiety*

(Experience Zen Miracle Now)

Joseph Tolle

Published by Robert Satterfield Publishing House

© Joseph Tolle

Meditation: Self Development Guide For Peace,
Mindfulness and Kundalini Awakening and Expand Your
Subconscious Mind Power To Beat Anxiety

(Experience Zen Miracle Now)

ISBN 978-1-989682-65-4

This document is geared towards providing exact and reliable information in regards to the topic and issue covered. The publication is sold with the idea that the publisher isn't required to render accounting, officially permitted, or otherwise, qualified services. If advice is necessary, legal or even professional, a practiced individual in the profession should be ordered.

- From a Declaration of Principles which was accepted and approved equally by a Committee of the American Bar Association and a Committee of Publishers and Associations.

The information provided herein is stated to be truthful and consistent, in that any liability, in terms of inattention or otherwise, by any usage or abuse of any policies, processes, or directions contained within is the solitary and also utter responsibility of the recipient reader. Under no

TABLE OF CONTENTS

Chapter 1: Understanding Meditation And Its Benefits

Before we discuss how to meditate, let us start out by discussing what meditation really is and how it can help transform your life.

Understanding Meditation

Meditation is a practice that induces a state of deep inner peace and awareness. It clarifies your thoughts and makes you aware of your surroundings. Meditation is not just a few seconds of silence that you and I sometimes have or deliberately practice. In fact, it is much more than those few moments of silence.

Meditation is the profound and eventual peace that comes after we let our mind gradually stop its persistent activity while it is fully aware.

Meditation calms your racing mind; it does so by making you focus on one thing at a time. When you learn to focus better on things, you ultimately learn how to silence your racing mind and concentrate on what is important.

Moreover, meditation works to stabilize your different brainwave states. How does it do that? Well, let me explain. Your brain operates within the confines of the 5 brainwave states: gamma, beta, alpha, theta, and delta with gamma being the most active and delta being the calmest one.

When you are actively thinking and planning things, your brain operates in the gamma or beta brainwaves. If stimulated too much, these brainwaves can bring about anxiety and stress.

Why Meditate?

Meditation has countless benefits. Let's examine a few of them in closer detail.

1: Attainment of Internal Peace and Clarity of Mind

Meditation is popular all around the world for being an exercise that cultivates mental clarity and internal peace. How does meditation bring clarity and peace? That's simple: meditation is a process of slowing down your thought process, something that gradually helps you dismiss negative thoughts.

When you can discard negative thoughts that keep your mind busy and cluttered, your mind becomes very clear and your thoughts become positive. When your mind is clear, you start focusing on your priorities and start focusing more on the blessing that is your everyday life.

2: Helps Reduce Stress

Meditation also reduces your mental noise and gradually silences your inner critic/self that distracts you from the right path. It helps you relax your body while controlling your breathing.

When you simultaneously control the noise and your breathing, you easily replace the anxiety residing inside you with a sense of peace you have never experienced before. When the anxiety decreases and when your mind becomes focused and clear, you feel less stressed and more peaceful.

3: Helps You Practice Self-Acceptance and Self-Love

Meditation also helps you practice self-acceptance and self-love with greater ease. Self-acceptance refers to accepting and acknowledging yourself wholly, and self-love means loving yourself better.

Meditation helps you overcome unhealthy thinking patterns that drive you towards self-hate. Naturally, when you eliminate such thoughts from your mind, you become more accepting of yourself, which consequently helps you love yourself more.

4: Increases your Confidence levels

Meditation helps you train your mind to remain rational and act appropriately. How does it do that? Well, it disconnects you from negative and inappropriate thoughts that decrease your confidence. When these negative and critical thoughts tarnish your self-esteem, you start negatively judging yourself, which consequently decreases your confidence to invariably low levels.

Meditation not only helps you disconnect from harmful thoughts, it also makes you feel more in control of your body, emotions, and judgments. Having this control helps you become much more confident.

In addition, meditation helps improve your immune system, health, emotional well-being, creativity, relationships, and overall quality of life. To learn more about the benefits of meditation, you can go here.

Now that you know what meditation is, and what it can do for you, let us move on to the next chapter to understand how you can practice it.

Chapter 2: Quick Meditation Techniques To Thwart Anxiety

Science proves that shallow breathing is one of the biggest causes of anxiety. When you feel nervous about something, your fight or flight response, which is your usual stress response, becomes active. This response leads to different physiological changes including shallow breathing. Shallow breathing refers to taking short, rapid breaths. Shallow breathing makes you even more anxious, stressed and depressed. Thus, the first step to dealing with this is practicing deep breathing.

Below are a few quick meditation practices that can help you achieve that so you can break the biggest contributor to stress, anxiety, and forgetfulness.

How To Practice The Equal Breathing Meditation Technique

Known as 'sama vritti' in Sanskrit, equal breathing is a simple breathing exercise that helps you shift from shallow breathing to deep breathing. When you take slower, deep breaths, you find it easy to stay in the moment and become more mindful. Here is how you can practice it:

1.   Sit comfortably in a quiet place and inhale to a count of four.

2.   Exhale that breath to another count of four.

3.   Inhale and exhale through your nose.

4.   Do this for 2 to 5 minutes, and as you breathe, focus on your breath and nothing else so you train your mind to live in the moment.

You can practice this meditation technique at any time of the day. However, doing it first thing in the morning upon waking up and any time you feel a panic attack building up will work well in your favor.

How To Practice The Alternate Nostril Breathing Technique

This technique is perfect for restoring balance and calmness in both the right and left hemispheres of your brain so you always stay peaceful and can battle anxiety like a pro. To practice it, do the following:

1.   Sit comfortably in any pose you like, preferably with your crossed legs in the lotus or half lotus pose.

2.   Put the right thumb over the right nostril and take a deep in-breath through your left nostril.

3.   When your in-breath reaches its peak, close the left nostril using your ring finger and exhale via the right nostril.

4.   Continue breathing in this pattern—inhaling via your right nostril, closing it off with your right thumb, and exhaling via the left nostril.

5.   Practice this for 2 to 5 minutes or even 40 to 60 seconds if 2 or 5 minutes seems too much.

While you can practice this technique at any time, it works best when you do it any time when you want to energize and realign your focus. Since it heightens your sense of alertness and consciousness, it is best not to do it before bedtime or you will find yourself lying awake in bed for hours.

How To Practice Abdominal Breathing Technique

Abdominal breathing is yet another effective technique you can use to train yourself to breathe deeply. To practice it, do the following:

1.   Place one hand on your chest and the other on your belly.

2.   Inhale deeply through your nose and ensure your diaphragm fully inflates with air to the extent that you feel a stretch in your lungs.

3.   When you feel the stretch, release the breath.

4.   Take 5 to 10 deep breaths using this procedure.

Breathe in this manner for at least 2 to 3 times daily and in about 3 to 4 weeks, you will find yourself taking slow, deep breaths more often and feeling calmer than before. To nurture a habit of these practices, practice them repeatedly throughout the day. You can practice all of them or pick the one you like best and do it repeatedly. Soon, you will be breathing deeply whenever you are awake, which means you will stay aware of yourself and everything around you.

To further increase your sense of calmness and mindfulness, try mindfulness meditation. The next chapter discusses this.

Chapter 3: Types Of Meditation

In the previous two chapters, we read about the history and benefits of meditation respectively. In this one we will read on the different forms of meditation. There are many forms of meditation that you can take up and they are as under.

Kundalini meditation

Kundalini meditation is the art of balancing the chakras in your body. The human body consists of 7 chakras that are placed in the center of the body. This form of meditation helps in cleansing and balancing the chakras and assists in increasing your happiness. This capitalizes on focusing over the different elements inside the body, which we read about in chapter 1.

To perform: Start by assuming the lotus pose. Draw in a few deep breaths. Now imagine a small ball of light originating from your first chakra and then moving up to your second. This then moves to the third, then the fourth, the fifth, the sixth and lastly the seventh. The ball of light then pierces through your aura chakra located on top of you head. Continue imagining this for 15 minutes. You must imagine that the ball of light is getting bigger with every successful upward move and is collecting all the undesirable elements from your body before leaving with it. We will look at the various chakras in detail in the next chapter.

Qi Gong

Qi gong is a type of mediation that is a lot like kundalini mediation. The basic intent is to cleanse the chakras inside the body so that the mind and body work well in tandem with each other. But don't think of taking up any one of these alone, as they are both equally beneficial in their own right. This is just as simple to perform as the kundalini form of meditation.

To perform: To perform this meditation; start by sitting in the lotus pose. Draw in a few deep breaths. Now imagine a small ball of fresh air originating from your base chakra. This ball then moves to your fourth chakra and remains there for a couple of seconds. Then it moves to the last chakra situated inside your head and remains there. The ball then moves back to your fourth chakra and from there, back to your first chakra. It keeps doing this to create a cosmic circuit inside your body. The ball of air nourishes all the organs that it comes into contact with. You can also imagine a ball of fresh water that is cleaning your internal system.

Yoga meditation

As was mentioned in chapter 1, yoga and meditation are related to each other. There are certain yoga based breathing exercises that are meant to be carried out as meditational practices. Let us look at them in detail.

Pranayama

Pranayama is the easiest form of breathing meditation and is performed as under.

To perform: Start by assuming the lotus pose. Draw in a few deep breaths and relax your body. Now place your right thumb over your right nostril and inhale through your left. Hold the breath for a few seconds and free your right nostril while covering your left with your index finger. Exhale through your right. Now draw in a breath from your right again and exhale through your left. Keep this motion going and remain as calm as possible. Continue for 5 minutes and gradually increase the time to 15 minutes after a week's practice.

Kapalbhati

Kapalbhati is a fast breathing technique meant to help you eliminate impurities from your body.

To perform: to perform this technique, start by sitting in the lotus pose and draw in a few deep breaths. Now start exhaling at a fast pace so that you exhale faster than you inhale. Do this for 3 minutes and then increase to 10 minutes gradually.

Sama vritti

Sama vritti is another form of breathing meditation that is commonly practiced. Here is how you can perform it.

To perform: start by sitting in the lotus pose. Sama stands for equal and vritti stands for breathing. So draw in a deep breath to the count of 4 and then exhale to a count of 4. Next count to 6 and then to 8 and then to 10! Remember to breathe equally and not vary the intensity.

Bhrastrika

Bhrastrika pranayama is an advanced form of breathing technique. Here is how to perform it.

To perform: start by assuming the lotus pose. Now close your eyes and draw in a couple of deep breaths. When you wish to exhale, swoon down and lift your head up while exhaling. Do this for 2 minutes and then increase to 5. If you feel dizzy then stop immediately.

It is best to perform these one after the other and spend 40 to 45 minutes.

Mindfulness meditation

Mindfulness meditation is a great meditational technique to adopt. It is a simplistic form of meditation yet extremely effective. In fact, it is one of the most important aspects of mindfulness and helps you increase your concentration power. You can easily adopt this technique and can be performed as under.

To perform: start by preparing for the meditation. Look for an object that makes for a calming sight. This can be the image of Buddha or a plant with a flower. Now sit in front of it a little distance. Assume the lotus pose and draw in deep breaths. Close your eyes 3/4ths and stare at the object in front of you. Don't frown when you do so and free the muscles in your face. You can also smile or have a big grin on your face, like Buddha, when you perform this technique. You must mindfully concentrate on the object lying in front of you alone and cut out everything else from around you.

Heart rhythm meditation

Heart rhythm meditation is a very relaxing and rejuvenating form of meditation. Heart rhythm meditation is meant to help you align your mind and body and also invigorate your soul. Heart rhythm meditation is fairly easy to perform.

To perform: to perform this technique start by sitting in a relaxing pose. It is not important for you to sit in the lotus pose and can also sit on a chair if that is comfortable. Now close your eyes and draw in a few deep breaths. Place your right hand over your heart and identify your heartbeats. Establish a pattern. Now imagine your heart pumping in fresh blood and imagine it flowing through your hand and going to the other parts of your body. Next, imagine it travelling to your brain and nourishing it completely. Imagine that each cell in your body is feeling completely fresh and invigorated.

Hypnosis

Hypnosis is a meditational technique meant to induce a trance. A trance is a state of mind where you go into a state of subconscious. You will have to travel to your subconscious mind and explore whatever lies there. This is also a form of meditation and is meant to help you tap into your problems and identify them so that you can correct them.

To perform: to perform this, start by assuming the lotus pose. If you find the bed comfortable then you can rest on it. But don't fall asleep. Now close your eyes and try to travel to your subconscious. Focus on the thoughts that you feel are emanating from the back of your head. Understand what they mean. You will successfully be in a state of subconscious if you follow these steps.

Guided visualization

Guided visualization is similar to the hypnosis technique. This is a form of meditation that is great for people looking to increase their physical strength and fight an illness effectively. Guided visualization is simple to perform but leaves you feeling rejuvenated.

To perform: Start by sitting in the lotus pose, or you can also lie down on a sofa or a bed. Sleep calmly and draw in deep breaths. Now place your hands over your chest and interlock the fingers. Close your eyes and visualize yourself sleeping in an open field with soft green grass, where the bright sun is shining upon your face. The fresh breeze is blowing over you and you have not a care in this world. You are completely relaxed and any bodily issue that you have has left you for good. You don't have any problems and are enjoying life in the field.

Zazen

Zazen is a form of movement-based meditation that is meant to help you get some physical activity into your meditation routine. It is fairly easy to perform and will leave you feeling relaxed.

To perform: to perform this technique start by choosing an appropriate place. Now sit with your legs folded and place your butt over the backs of your feet. Look straight and focus on something that lies in front of you. Now start moving forward and back like a pendulum. You must maintain a steady motion and move at a constant speed. Don't get into a jerky motion and try to remain as focused on your posture as possible. You can perform this for 5 minutes and then increase to 15 minutes.

Walking meditation

The next type of meditation is known as walking meditation. This is also a movement-based meditation that you can try out.

To perform: to perform this meditation, pick a place where you can walk in a straight line. There should be enough space for you to walk front, turn and walk back. Stand at the starting point and place your right leg forward. Inhale while doing so. Next, place your left leg forward and exhale. Keeps this motion going until you feel tired. You can also turn around in circles if you like. Traditionally, a gong is made use of to know when to place your feet forward. You can make use of an alarm or get someone to hit a singing bowl for you as an indication. The bowl will further add to your meditational practice.

These from the different meditational techniques that you can adopt, and exploit, on a day-to-day basis

Chapter 4: How To Use Guided Meditations To Battle Stress And Depression

Guided meditations are an incredible tool for anyone who meditates.

Whether you are new to meditation or have been meditating for years, you should most certainly know the power and benefits you can gain from following a guided meditation.

As you learn more techniques to bring yourself into a meditative state you will probably want to start using guided meditations. A guided meditation is an exercise that is perfect in relieving the daily stress you are facing by simply learning how to concentrate and focus long enough to get a few minutes of peaceful relaxation.

The Effects Of Guided Meditations

You will feel a sense of calmness overcome you and it will make the rest of your day go smoother. Following a Guided meditation only take a few minutes and they can easily be done after you have enjoyed your lunch and before heading back into the daily grind. It is a proven method of bringing the world back into order and making you feel less stressed by the things going on around you.

Psychologists Recommend Using Guided Meditations

Guided meditations have been so successful in helping people through stressful situations that many physicians have actually prescribed these exercises to patients who suffer from anxiety attacks and depression from being under such overwhelming stress and a sense of hopelessness. They are also extremely helpful for increasing self-awareness, self-love, and self-confidence.

Meditating makes it much easier for you to cope with the stresses that daily life may throw at you. They have proven to be so powerful that many mental health patients have been able to go off of their medications and move on to being more productive members of society in every aspect of their lives by following a guided meditation on a daily and regular basis.

There is no doubt that any style of meditation is a helpful form of treatment for the body and the mind.

When a person is dealing with their everyday mind, they are distracted by things as mundane as their pets to the more stressful aspects of their professional working career. A person cannot relax or maintain an even keel so to speak when the mind is in this much turmoil. The stress continues to build until the mind finally shuts down due to overwhelming exhaustion. A mind that is concentrated is more centered and focused but it is still dealing with the distractions of everyday life. It makes it hard for a person to be able to meditate without going back to the distractions that were plaguing them in the first place.

Using Guided Meditation For Reducing Stress

Life can become ⍰uite exhausting when you suffer from mental stress. Even the smallest tasks seem difficult and overwhelming leaving you tired from the effort. Mental tension can be a joy killer, taking all the pleasure and fun out of daily living. It is a sad state to fall into; however, it need not be a permanent state. Once you recognize some of the symptoms of this affliction, you can begin efforts to overcome its effects and regain your joy of living.

Guided meditation truly is a remarkable tool for reducing stress and helping you connect with your inner peace and spirituality. While people use guided meditation for everything from healing and clearing anger to managing chronic pain and learning to forgive, we'll focus here on reducing stress with guided meditation audios.

Meditation takes us to a calm, serene place to eliminate harmful stress from the body. Meditation truly has the ability to restore and heal the mind and body. If you struggle to deal with stress from your daily life and work, you may feel like it's just impossible to actually let go and relax in meditation. That's how guided meditation, or guided imagery, helps you discover this inner peace on your own.

While traditional meditation involves stilling your mind and body, guided meditation is about going on a visualized journey. With a guided imagery meditation, a guide directs you through the process to bring you encouragement, peace and other tools for success in your life by talking you through the process in a smoothing voice with imagery to assist you.

You simply listen to your guide and let his or her words and images guide you through the meditation process and let your imagination follow along. In many cases, meditation music is included, or nature sounds, which aid in the relaxation process. As you focus, the regular world will slowly fade away, calming your mind and helping you slip into a state of deep relaxation.

Guided meditation is especially helpful for reducing stress as this journey gives you a temporary escape from your daily worries and recharges your mind and body, preparing you for a new day and giving you the inner calm you need to face the world with light and joy.

To get the most benefit from any guided meditation CD you choose, it's best to go somewhere comfortable where you can sit in peace for 15 minutes. Make sure all distractions like the television and phone are turned off then relax in your favorite chair. It's best to use headphones while listening to a guided imagery CD so you can focus on the journey, rather than any minor distracting noises in the room. Close your eyes and breathe deeply for a few minutes before your guide helps you enter that state of relaxation.

There are many benefits to using this effective form of relaxation program which, by the way, is currently being used to help firefighters manage one of the country's most high-stress careers.

1. Guided meditation programs offer the benefits of meditation to you with convenience and comfort in your own home. You gain a personal guide who helps you navigate into a deep state of peace and relaxation at any time you like. This is especially important given how busy our lives can become.

2. Guided meditation CDs are often seen as the best way to learn meditation for beginners because you have an experienced healer bringing you powerful images to help your mind relax and transport your imagination to another realm.

3. Guided imagery is also very easy to use, whether you've never tried meditation before or you've been doing it for years. It's especially helpful if you have trouble focusing because the audio guide keeps your mind engaged. This helps your subconscious slip into that peaceful state necessary for true relaxation and healing.

The Mental Stress Traps

The reasons people fall under mental or psychological stress varies with the individual. Some people succumb to pressures in their workplace due to work overload, too many timely deadlines to meet, not getting along with their boss or colleagues, lack of skill or knowledge to accomplish their tasks, complications in assigned projects, competition, etc. Other people may experience stress due to family affairs - arguments with siblings, children or spouse; disagreements over financial matters; sickness or death in the family, etc. We live in an extremely stressful world surrounded by stressful people and situations. However, we can learn to rise above these situations, find solutions to our problems and overcome tension and fear in our lives.

The Effects of Psychological Stress

Nervous tension affects people negatively in different ways, physically and mentally. Mental effects may include lack of focus and concentration, lack of sleep, inexplicable fears, tension, irrationality, anger, indecision, moodiness, etc. Physical effects may range from headaches and migraines to problems with digestion, ulcers, strokes, heart attack, dizziness, nausea and more. Though there are many treatments and medications you can try to help relieve these symptoms, more and more people today are discovering how they can overcome stress using meditation.

Guided Meditation For Relaxation

Meditation provides a natural means of reducing the strain and pressures in your life, especially when practiced on a regular basis. The simple process of taking time from your busy schedule regularly to meditate on the positive aspects of your life, enjoy creation, listen to faith building stories and ⏃uotations, relax with your favorite music and enter into a state of peace and rest can eliminate tension and fear. During this time you are focusing your mind and heart on that which is good and positive and uplifting. You refuse to allow negative thoughts and emotions to build up and overpower you. You learn to look for and be thankful for the good, count your blessings and dwell on the positive aspects of your situation. By dwelling on the positive, you maintain peace of mind and spirit which in turn enables you to find solutions to the problems you face.

Meditation has been tried and proven to help reduce stress. It is a simple process to put into practice and can help you live a more enjoyable life. You can start incorporating meditation into your life today and reap the positive results of a more peaceful, happy existence.

Important Statistics About Stress

77% of people in the United States experience physical or psychological symptoms of stress, including muscle tension, appetite changes, headaches and irritability, and one third of people feel they live with an extreme level of stress. Half of adults feel their stress has a negative impact on their work or personal life, which includes fights with friends or families members or sleep problems. It's also estimated that stress accounts for $300 billion annually in costs for employers in terms of both stress-related health care and missed days at work. Finally, the American Psychological Association warns that stress is a major problem in the United States that needs to be addressed.

Path To Physical And Mental Well-Being

If stress and anxiety are taking over your life, you should get help of guided meditation as your stress management resource. Learn how to meditate and free your mind of worries in order to lead a healthy and peaceful life.

The high-speed lifestyle that all of us lead today doesn't leave us much of choice other than juggling a number of tasks. Some of your time is spent enlisting the jobs that are needed to be done, some carrying out the jobs and the rest in worrying about the ones that you weren't able to finish. All this leaves you stressed out. Meditation is a great way to shift your focus from anxiety to peace. It is a complementary medicine that cures all three, mind, body and soul of a person.

Meditation can help you release stress and lead a happy and peaceful life.

By providing a state of relaxation, it helps you remove the troubled thoughts that cloud your mind and cause stress. Moreover, it helps you focus your attention resulting in improved physical and metal well-being. Studies have found that meditation is beneficial in treating various health conditions that are worsened by stress. Some of them are high blood pressure, chronic pain, fatigue, sleeping habits, depression and others. Furthermore, it also helps you control your anger and anxiety.

When you meditate, all your tensions seem to go away. Releasing stress isn't just limited to the meditation session, it gradually eliminates the stress from your life given that you practice it on a regular basis. The true profoundness of meditation lies in the stability that you develop overtime. It helps you lead a life that remains unperturbed by anxiety and stress. Though difficulties will still come along at times, you will be able to handle them with much ease and won't be troubled by negative thoughts.

The technique of meditation requires much practicing and can be mastered overtime. For learning to meditate, however, you need the guidance of an expert. Searching online is the easiest way to find an experienced meditation practitioner. There are some experts who provide online podcast about meditation. From teaching you the basics as well as the latest findings on meditations, helping you achieve a relaxed state of mind to guided meditations for listening while you meditate, they share expert tips and help you find what works best for you to release tension.

Listening to a podcast is so much a better option for learning to meditate than reading about it. During a meditation podcast, you are guided by the soothing voice of a meditation expert to help you relax. Since your mind needs reason to be calm and peaceful, it should be preferred if someone guides you, taking your mind off the worries and helping you find inspiration to feel fresh and relaxed. You need someone who holds years of experience in meditation to free you of your stress.

Chapter 5: Health Is The Greatest Gift, Contentment The Greatest Wealth, Faithfulness The Best Relationship

Buddha

Putting it into practice in the real world is the true learning of meditation. In fact, of any learning. No point having the knowledge if you cannot apply it in your life.

Have you ever done some course and felt it changed your life only to return home and find the same, same old ensues. Whatever enthusiasm you had lost.

I need to tell you something, it may come as a shock or perhaps it will make sense.

We are no different to the dog that barks at the cat or the cat that chases the mouse.

We are triggered to react based on our past experiences. It is the only way the mind learns how hot things hurt and is for our safety but when emotions get involved then your poor mind views every position trigger as life threatening which isn't but your mind cannot differentiate.

Triggers for anxiety, stress, anger, depression will be people, places or situations and all three need to be recognized so more appropriate responses can be learned and used.

A tone of voice, a person's demeanor, a physical room will all trigger either unpleasant or happy memories and your body reacts accordingly.

The smell of freshly baked bread transports me to my grandmother's kitchen and a feeling of love. Whereas a dismissive attitude towards me used to trigger my anger.

Mindful meditation preparation which will work in the following situations:

- work,

- social,

- family.

Exercise:

As this requires times to learn how to do it, there is no shortened version. The more times you practice, the more adept you become. I want you to establish the feelings of positive and negative and then how you can manage the negative feelings by interrupting the cycle.

It takes three positive thoughts to cancel a negative thought.

To begin, as before:

Find a place where you can relax.

Meditation music of your choice.

Allow your body to become limp and relaxed.

Notice your thoughts, let them float by as you observe them.

Recall a happy memory from your past. Be there. See what you see, feel what you feel. Notice how all of your senses engage. Perhaps you are smiling.

Notice where this good feelings lives inside you, it is your head, your chest, maybe all over.

Observe you, how do you look? What is your facial expression? How do you hold your body?

This is the relaxed and happier you.

Recall another memory. Be in that memory.

Recall another memory. Be in that moment.

See you in this memory, happier, more at ease.

If you've never experienced happiness, what is the closest thing to it you have experienced and do as above. Or what do you imagine happiness to be like?

Work Stress:

Who or what causes you stress at work? How do you show up? What is your demeanor?

What if could swap your relaxed self for your work self? Make the appropriate changes and adjustments.

Notice the difference it makes. How much better does it feel?

What do you need to do to be this person?

Notice how by adjusting your disposition, enables you to choose whether to respond or not at all.

The irrate person on the phone, create a protective bubble around your so their vile just slides off you. Sit upright, don't lean over onto your desk or raise your head up. If you absorb their negativity, it becomes part of you. Don't give them that power.

The manager that doesn't seem to like you. As they complain and shout at you, see yourself in your bubble perhaps you are on a beach or back in a happy thought. Let their venom slide off you. If you absorb their negativity, it becomes part of you. Don't give them that power.

The meeting that you dread attending. How can you change it up? Sing your favorite song inside your head. Music relaxes us and has the power to transport us back to a time in our lives when we were free from stress. Go into the room all pumped up, your body relaxed and notice how others are stressed. If you can, choose a different position than usual.

By creating minor adjustments inside, you produce phenomenal improvements on the outside.

Social Stress:

Remember the venue is irrelevant. Why are you meeting with your friends, to catch up, have fun? If doesn't seem to be true, then get new friends.

What makes you a good friend? Don't list the qualities of a being a labrador.

You need to become part of the group. Notice how in the past you always seem to be on the outside, now go into the middle of the group.

Relax your face and body.

Listen to the conversation. Be present.

If shy, we have a tendency to sit back, to want others to include us but from another's perspective, this may be viewed as wanting to be left alone!

As you see yourself, ensure your feet are in line with your body. Anxiety and stress create the fight or flight response and your feet will point towards the nearest exit!

What does having fun mean to you? What do you want your memories to be when you get home?

Family Stress:

Perhaps the most difficult of all. They know our triggers, our weaknesses. Taking what you have learned, begin this exercise with the situation that causes you some mild stress and from here, you will build to the higher stress triggers.

Begin with a happy memory. See yourself being happy, connect to that feeling inside you.

How do you sound? Try lowering your voice. Women have a tendency to become more high pitched, lowering your voice gives you more confidence immediately.

Feeling your colors get stronger inside, become more grounded. Imagine a protective bubble around you, keeping calm in and negativity out. You are in control of your emotions.

Noticing weakness and a return of your anger, anxiety or whatever emotion is provoked. Interrupt its progress. Meditate on your breathing, step away if you have to (not run), in order to compose yourself. Give permission for the feeling to go, to change.

Run through the exercise again. Make adjustments accordingly.

Each time you run through these scenarios, notice how much stronger you feel within yourself.

Now putting it into practice. This begins as soon as you notice the stress alert going off inside yourself.

With mindful meditation, you are fully aware but able to "see" how you want to be in the situations that have previously provoked.

Preparation is key.

Interrupt the physical manifestation of stress — slow your breathing, relax your shoulders.

Interrupt the thoughts - "I am in control", "I can do this".

Chapter 6: Benefits Of Meditation

Physical body benefits:

Sleep

Sleep is one of the top 5 factors of good health (physical and mental). Many people have sleep problems. Problem like when

•   They feel their body is tired and their body needs a deep sleep to get refreshed or healthy again.

•   Many people get into habit of thinking about their office work or official conversation, which creates stress just before sleeping which can delay sleep or creates shallow sleep.

•   Many people can't sleep quickly even when they are on bed for hours.

• On other hand come people feels sleepy during their work time. This is just the effect of people not getting good and deep sleep during night.

Most of the above symptoms are caused by work stress, distraction, and emotional roller coaster, together with untimely sleeping habit.

Here how Meditation help is as you have also figured out in chapter 1 "What is Meditation", mediation creates barrier between your daily stress emotional roller coaster , thus you are unaffected by all these reason which causes these sleep disorder symptoms. Mind is calm and peaceful though-out the day. As during meditation you will gets to know that thoughts, stress, emotions comes and go in your mind, one should get attached to them. One should analysesthem in detach mode and take positive decision in life. This ways one's inner self is always at peace and sleep comes quicker and deeper for him/her.

One can mediate just before sleep for 5 mins to 15 mins to get maximum benefits.

Weight and Energy

One body weight and energy level should be optimum and a healthy life. Understand that your body is just a tool given by God to accomplish your worldly tasks. If these tools are not in perfect condition, it affects life and your productivity. Obesity and Low energy are one of major health problem people are suffering today. These problems can affect one's relationship, social life, and financial life indirectly.

Obesity and low energy are generally caused by person's unawareness of some food habits. Caused by certain food addictions like sugar, alcohol etc .

Here why Meditation is useful because it help to focus in youmore and more. It strength one's analysis power. One starts understanding his/her body better. One gets more aware of things which are important to one's body and which are not.

You may naturally starts feeling that Vegetables and fruits are more suitable to your body than fast foods/junk food. Which is the truth also..

You may start feeling alcohol, cigarette smoking, and sugar addiction only make you feel good for small amount of time and then you go into depression state or craving state.

Sooner or later one automatically start leaving these bad habits because this feeling comes from inside, not from outside (from your friends, family etc.).

And one starts focusing on good habits which are beneficial for one'body.

Obesity and low energy are primarily caused by these bad food habits. So Meditation hits the root cause of these habits and helps in eliminating them.

One may find different ways to lose weight and gain energy like strict diet, rigorous exercise , pills etc and those will be temporary and effect will only be there until you do these things (until you exercise , until you take pills) .

However Meditation hits the roots cause of these habits and habits naturally leave leaves the person rather person leaves the habits.

Other health benefits

- Improves Immune system

- Decrease Ageing.

- Regulate breathing and heart rate.

- Reduces blood pressure

- Increases Longevity

- Increases energy level and decreases fatigue.

- Reduces bad effect of any chronic body pain on physical body and on emotional state.

- Decreasing of muscular tension , stress and headaches

- Help in Arthritis, inflammatory disorder and asthma.

Mental benefits:

Positivity in Life:

With consistence practice of meditation, once mind becomes more calm and peaceful. Meditation increased once clarity in mind. It increased once ability to focus . Focus on anything increasesthat thing in your life. Positive or negative. If once focus on negative thoughts,"I am not capable of doing it","I am poor"etc. . That same things increase in his/her life. If one focus on positive,"Why I cannot do this", "Why not I can become rich in my life","I can do whatever is needed to become rich and fulfilled", then those things increase in life. With Meditation you understand things as it is and focus on positive more and more.

It's a Stress and Anxiety buster:

I very act of recognition that your thoughts come and go through your mind, reduce our stress and anxiety drastically. You are not your thought but your thoughts are part of you.

Time spend with one's self during meditation, help to be unaffected by outside world and love self. Meditation can help you to popup your problem to come on surface so that you can take better decision to resolve them, rather then stressing-out because of them.

There is Buddhist saying that"Answers come in still mind". Mediation helps to still/clam your mind so that you can listen to your soul more clearly.

Emotional balance and harmony with nature:

Meditation removes unnecessary negatives thought from one's mind. Nourishes it with positive thoughts. It clams the mind, by making us neutral so that we are not depressed in unfavorable condition or do not get overexcited or overwhelmed in favorable condition. So it helps to keep a balance emotionally.

Meditation helps to understand that we are just a part of this whole universe and we cannot live without making harmony with nature. If we live unharmoniously it will only affect our self negatively not the nature or universe.

Meditation also helps us to accept the circumstances and things as they are. Stress, anger, anxiety,sorrow comes when you don't see things as they are, you expect those things, you want to be. If you start understanding and accepting things as they are, you will be free from sorrow, stress, anger and anxiety. Mediation helps in achieving this.

Other mental benefits of meditation are:

1.   Improve memory.

2.   resolve phobia's and fears

3.   Controls Anger.

4.   Develop Intuition.

5.   Increase concentration.

6.   Helps is quitting addictions.

7.   Decrease in potential mental illness.

8.   Prevent and potentially cure depression.

9.   Decreases restless thinking and worrying.

10.   Improves relationships.

11.   Improves productivity.

12.   Helps one to focus more on important things in life rather than just wasting time of our life.

Spiritual benefits:

As you might now able to understand that meditation clams your mind from unnecessary thinking and help ones to becomes closure to one's soul. , thus increase your spiritual world.

It helps one to be in more harmony with nature and existence. Help to understand that there is big power behind all existence, the GOD.

As one spends time with himself during meditation it helps in self-actualization. One starts understanding oneself. What is good and what is bad habits in him and can rectify them.

Meditation helps increase in growing wisdom. One starts understanding life in much better and clear ways.

It helps in increasing happiness, compassion, and forgiveness,increase sense of"oneness", decrease ego and helps in discovering purpose in life. All these make one free from materialistic bondage and make him/her truly free.

Chapter 7: Making Meditation A Part Of Your Daily Life

"I don't have the time to meditate!" This is the most common thing I hear while I am sharing my experiences about meditation with people I know. I am sure you too would be thinking of saying the same thing. It's perfectly normal. I too had the same reaction before starting off. You are so caught up with the routine that you tend to just go with the flow without thinking. You seem to be so busy with work, kids, laundry, groceries and cooking that you have no time for anything.

The answer to this is simple — Start Meditating Today! It cannot get more real than this. If you are the kind who just cannot find the time to meditate, my message for you is — Make time for

Meditation! You have to make meditation a priority in your life.

When I had my first kid, I used to find it really tough to stick to the meditation schedule that I set for myself. I was more of a nocturnal animal who had to attend to the needs of my newborn, leaving me completely drained out by morning. Meditation seemed far-fetched because I was far from being patient. As days passed I started getting anxious as I wasn't really able to connect with myself midst all the chaos. Slowly and steadily, I started figuring out ways to incorporate meditation into my daily routine and now I can share with you simple steps that worked for me.

Like every human being, I chose the path of least resistance and came up with these easy steps that will enable you to include meditation in your life. I challenge you that with these steps, you can meditate anytime and anywhere — even when you partake in your routine chores. Gone are the days when you needed a meditation pillow and a few minutes in the morning to meditate. These tips will break that myth for you. Meditation can transcend in any facet of your life if you do it effectively and consistently. The following steps will take a lot of determination and dedication at your end.

1.   Make a Meditation Schedule and Stick with it: Decide on a time during the day when you find it comfortable to meditate and stick to it, come what may. Look at meditation like one of the 'must-dos' of the day. The biggest obstacle to this is you yourself. You will keep coming up with novel excuses to procrastinate

your meditative sessions. Don't give in to this temptation. Make it a habit. When you do that you will get accustomed to it and the comfort level will keep going up. Once you start, you will feel uneasy if you do not meditate. This happens with me often. Since meditation is a habit for me, I feel extremely out of place if I miss it even once. It's like brushing your teeth. Don't you feel filthy if you do not start your day by brushing or bathing?

My suggestion: No matter what time you are up in the morning, meditate for 15 minutes. Start your day with meditation. Once you start, dedicate that time for it every single day. In case you have some unavoidable task to perform, you can always reschedule your session.

2.   Be Creative: Meditation is primarily concentrating on your thoughts while not letting your mind wander away. Sometimes think differently. Think out-of-the-box as to how you can incorporate meditation in everything you do.

☐   Meditate while brushing your teeth: Focus on what you are doing. Look at yourself in the mirror with a gentle smile and remind yourself of how you want to take care of every part of your body. Don't rush through brushing and rinsing. Instead, do it slowly and gently while contemplating on what you are doing.

☐   Meditate while You Drive: I definitely don't mean that you should close your eyes or not pay attention to the traffic on the road. Instead, be calm and aware of all the things around you. Keep your mobile on a silent mode and drive in complete silence. Don't let other drivers and the excessive traffic on the road bother you. Look around with a calm mind and be aware of all that's happening without reacting.

☐ Meditate at Work: Be mindful of your workplace. Keep interacting with colleagues and responding to emails in a patient and calm manner. Practice responding to a situation rather than reacting. When you do this, your colleagues and mail recipients will also be able to experience your state of mind. Contemplate on your thoughts, words and action while at work.

☐ Meditate while Exercising: Allow meditation to be a part of your life while you exercise. So instead of watching a movie while exercising, concentrate on each and every muscle you are working out on. Pay attention to each move you make and how it is playing a role in improving the blood circulation in your body. Concentrate on how the workout is nourishing every cell in your body.

☐ Meditate while Cooking: Cooking can be very therapeutic in itself. When my mother makes something with a lot of positive emotions and love, I can feel it. So while you are cooking, let go of any anxieties and fears. Think of all the nourishment you are about to provide to your loved ones through this food. Pay close attention to every ingredient you are adding. Shun every negative emotion and think of passing on your love and care to your family through this meal.

3. Keep a Dedicated Place for Meditation: A quiet and peaceful place is essential for a successful meditative session. Dedicate an area in your house or in a park nearby to meditate. Ensure you are not distracted by anything in the place you choose. Also, check for enough space around you so that you can seat yourself comfortably. If you are dedicating a room in your house, make sure it is devoid of distractions like the television, radio or a music system.

4. Simply Breathe: There are thousands of books talking about 'asanas' and breathing techniques to attain a meditative state. Don't get too technical. Just keep it simple and do what works for you. Just start off with some mindful breathing. This means you need to focus on your breathing. This has 3 distinct benefits:

☐ It calms you down instantly and helps you concentrate on your current state.

☐ It is very basic and easy. Everyone who wants to live breathes! All I am suggesting is to pay close attention to your breathing. You will not have to wait for long to get into a meditative state by doing this simple activity.

☐ You can breathe anywhere and anytime.

5. Practice Mindfulness in Your Regular Life too: Don't just wait for a meditative session to practice mindfulness. When you practice it in everything you do, you

become a changed person. You are more calm and patient. You are at peace with yourself and find solutions to problems rather than complaining about them. Make it a daily habit and see how it changes your personality. The more you are exposed to a particular thing the more you start accepting it as a part of you. It becomes your way of life. Moreover, you will fascinate others around you with your positive aura. They will want to know the secret behind your happy and calm mind.

6.   Resolve to Meditate Twice a day: Just like you do in the morning, practice meditation before you go to bed. The length of time you practice it for is completely based on your comfort level. If you find it tough to sit for 20 minutes at a stretch, split it into 2 different slots of 10 minutes each.

I am sure that if you incorporate these steps in your life, you will be able to incorporate meditation into your life effortlessly.

Chapter 8: Major Types Of Mediation

You may be wondering which type of meditation works best, but the answer will depend on your needs and preferences. There is no such thing as the most effective—what meditation type that works for you is just perfect.

The key here is finding the time and effort to sit each day to find that inner connection to self. If you are new to meditation, here are few of the many kinds that will best suit a beginner:

Guided Meditation

This is a type of meditation where there is a narrator that guides you to stimulate a certain change. In the beginning, you are assisted to relax your mind and body until you come deeper in your journey.

What's interesting is, the brain is not capable of differentiating a real event from those that you have imagined. Hence, performing guided mediation is comparable to real experiences, which produces a remarkable influence in your life.

How it Works?

Guided meditation is a prevailing way of provoking personal life changes, matched with how the brain functions. For instance, if you wish to excel in learning to play musical instruments, the brain has kept past experiences of you attempting to master a musical instrument. If you had bad experiences, the chances of mastering a musical instrument are low. On the other hand, if the experiences are good, the chances will be high.

What guided meditation does is to assist your brain reprogram itself by getting access to the subconscious part of the brain. The result is a better and new experience. The entire process is effortless, and highly enjoyable.

After the meditation session, you will be going back to the normal state making you feeling rejuvenated and refreshed. It can last for as short as 5 minutes or may take 15 to 20 minutes depending on your preference.

Suggestions:

Guided meditation can be simply done by listening to recorded narration or music that allows you to meditate anytime, anywhere. The sound in the background allows you to go deeper and further relax.

You may also utilize the sounds of nature along with the sceneries associated with these—like the sound of birds and flowing river. You can do it however you want as long as the results are apparent.

Mindfulness Meditation

This is a popular form of meditation—it can be described as awareness of the things that are happening in your surroundings, including the sounds and sensations among other things.

In this type of meditation, you allow your mind to drift from one thought to another without staying focused on a single thing. For example, you can practice mindfulness meditation when you live in a noisy neighborhood where there are lots of screaming and other noises. With this, you do not actually block the noises, but you are making yourself aware of that these distractions existed without turning your attention towards these.

In short, you are just being"mindful", letting your mind do the work. There are various techniques associated with this form of meditation, such as: mindful eating, deep breathing and sitting meditation among others.

Suggestion:

You may begin by taking position you feel comfortable with: sitting, standing, kneeling on a cushion. Remain in the position for minutes and be aware when your attention meander away. When this happens, just slowly bring it back to the surrounding and your body. The mind will always wander, and the most important thing here is to get it back gently.

Then, slowly focus your attention on your breathing—there is no certain way to breathe. Just let things flow naturally and don't worry about your breathing. If you stop worrying, your attention will be on the surrounding and your body.

Lastly, work your thoughts out. Experiencing overlapping thoughts is common, like what's is your schedule going to be like or that amazing movie trailer you just saw. When you notice that you have been so occupied with your thoughts, gently return to your breath and start over again.

This can be practiced for a period of 10 to 15 minutes or as long as 30 minutes or longer. Again, mindfulness mediation is not about halting the thinking process. Instead, it is about staying mindful of everything that occurs to the body and the environment.

Movement Meditation

This type of mediation may appear to challenging, but the experience can be too calming and rejuvenating once you get used to the practice. Not all people find this meditation suitable as they may feel comfortable just lying or sitting still.

However, there are also those who find it highly beneficial.

This meditation type involves gentle and repetitive movements to keep the mind and body occupied. It can be described as the act of silencing your mind while directing your entire focus to the things that you are doing at present.

Who Benefits the Most?

Well, this type of meditation is very helpful to those who are suffering from things like panic disorder, those who fall asleep when staying still for prolonged periods. It is also ideal for those who have disorders that hinder them from remaining still.

With this, the focus is on the mind, your breathing and also to the body movements. Remember, it is"moving meditation"and any form of movement can be considered as meditation if done slowly and with mindfulness.

In this, you focus on the environment and your body—your sensations, muscle movements, heart rate and other bodily activities.

There is also recognition of your body parts—be aware that they exist and make sure to assess and consider its value. For example, a body part that you dislike, like your nose that does not match the ideal can be re-incorporated to the body by being aware of its existence and significance.

Suggestion:

The most common technique in this form is"walking meditation", which provides the body with physical activity. At the same time, it also promotes good circulation and the elimination of physical tension. Here is how you can do it:

The best way is to match your breathing with your movements. Breathe naturally at a controlled or slow rate. Let your palms touch your chest and inhale slowly while extending your arms. While exhaling, return the palms to your chest. Feel the energy as you do this.

Stand up slowly, feel the lengthening of your body parts as you do this. Walk slowly forward and lengthen your legs in equal rates.

Then, sit down again in an expansive manner. Repeat the same movement while synchronizing the rhythm with your heartbeat. Do such movement with various levels of mental supervision.

This form of mediation is somehow therapeutic and may just like when focusing on your thoughts, objects, sounds etc.

Sensory Meditation

Most types of meditation involve the senses–movement and mindfulness meditation among others. Yet, meditation can be performed on senses alone.

Just like mindfulness meditation, sensory meditation can be performed on a daily basis. But mastery can be gained when you spend a few minutes each day to focus on your senses. With this, you can learn to live at the present, develop better perception and understanding of the body.

The key in this form of meditation is to focus your mind and senses on stimuli, like sounds, scents or objects etc. When you do, relaxation will come into the picture. Although you are using mind and senses, the results can be pretty amazing and rejuvenating.

Suggestion:

Perceive objects in a non-verbal manner–this is the case in most types of meditation. It is more like feeling, hearing, seeing instead of merely"thinking". In sensory mediation you enter a world where there is no comparison or identification, and there is no need to analyze or think.

Go to a relaxing place to exercise your senses to the fullest. This is where your sensory experience should go into action. For instance, getting a guitar to play music is simply a task, but feeling the chords and the sensations that are brought about by playing and the music is a rich sensory experience.

Spend a few minutes to hours daily to exercise sensory meditation without responding with it using your thoughts. You may also shift from one sensation to another—like from your sense of hearing to your sense of smell.

It is ideal to keep the eyes closed during the process to avoid possible distractions that may arise due to visual input.

Chapter 9: Is Meditation A Way To Find Peace Inside?

For millenniums, meditation had been used by various cultures of the world due to its numerous benefits, like:

• Finding peace inside;

• Improving attentiveness and relaxation;

• Relieving anxiety, unhappiness, pain, stress and insomnia; besides,

• Lessening tiredness.

When mixed with conservative medicine, it can improve bodily health, similar to heart wellness, rheumatologic disorders, and problems on digestion. In fact, the Mayo Clinic states, and I quote:

"There are many forms of meditation, but most have in common a quiet location, a specific comfortable posture and a focus of attention. The method often taught at Mayo Clinic is called paced-breathing meditation, which includes deep breathing."[1]

The different kinds of meditation include yoga; Tai Chi; Qi Gong; and, transcendental, guided, mantra, or mindfulness meditation. You could meditate formally or informally as you enjoy or as it matches your way of life and circumstances. You can do it within a group or by yourself.

The truth is, meditation is a communion with faith and self. Some persons incorporate meditation in their day to day routine, for instance, starting and ending a day through minutes of reflection. Here are several ways you could practice meditating by yourself whenever you wish:

1. Scanning the physique

When applying this system, focus your attention on the different parts of the human body one after another. Become conscious of the various feelings of every part of the body, whether that may be pain, stiffness, warmth, relief or rest.

2. Deep breathing

This method is perfect for newbies because inhalation and exhalation are normal functions. Simply focus your whole attention to your respiration. Concentrate on your feelings while listening to yourself breath through your nose. Inhale and exhale intensely and gradually. When your focus wanders, gradually return your attention to your taking breaths.

4. Mantra

You could create your personal mantra, may it be secular or religious. This can be observed using spiritual mantras, such as:

1.   "Our Father" in the Roman Catholic tradition[2];

2.   Holy designation of God in Judaism; and,

3.   "Om" or "Aum" mantras in Buddhism, Hinduism, and similar Eastern faiths.[3]

5. Walking while meditating

Combining walking with meditation exists as a well-organized and healthful way towards relaxing. You could use this practice anywhere and anytime you happen to be walking, irrespective of location. When you utilize this, hold back the speed of your walking and accordingly focus upon each motion of your feet and legs, as shown below.

6. Prayer

This is the finest known, as well as most practiced, model of meditating far and wide. Spoken, besides writing, devotions are established in the majority of faith customs. You could pray with your personal words or recite prayers penned by other people. Check out your neighborhood bookstore or surf the web for a standard to follow should you wish to write your own prayers. You may also consult your priest, pastor, rabbi or any spiritual head about potential resources.

7. Read or listen, then reflect

Many individuals claim that they gain much from understanding poems, motivating articles, or holy texts after taking some time, say three minutes, to silently reflect upon their import. You could likewise listen to revered music, verbalized words or a little instrumental music that you discover to be relaxing and inspiring.

8. Write down your reflections on love and gratitude

You can write down your thoughts in a personal journal or share them with friends. Focus these writings on your affection and thankfulness. In this meditation form, you can center your focus on a Supreme Entity or weave feelings of compassion, love and appreciation into your beliefs. After writing, read what you wrote, and then shut your eyes. Using the eyes of your mind, gaze at a peaceful scenery or representations of what you feel or aspire.

Chapter 10: Mindfulness

Before we begin with the actual steps of meditation, let's talk a little about the state of mind that you're adopting when you enter this activity. A vital part of any meditation is that of the development of mindfulness. The main goal here is to cultivate an awareness of your body.

You're probably not used to doing this. So the best warning is that as you become more aware of your body, your body will attempt to signal its discomfort with sitting still for any length of time. You may discover that you develop uncomfortable sensations or even pain in places you would never expect. Many complain of the urge to scratch themselves while they are practicing the stillness.

Don't allow this to upset or deter you because this is a normal part of the learning curve. It very well may be that these "sensations" were with you all the time, but you were just too busy to notice them.

That's why it's imperative that you choose a comfortable position for your meditative practice, especially when you're beginning. Just keep in mind that the small imperceptible physical feelings you normally have may become magnified during this period. And in many ways, this is a good sign. It means you're developing a greater sense of mindfulness.

Breathing

Breathing is the cornerstone of the meditative experience. If you go to India, it would be called Prana. It's closely related to life and energy — with good reason. Breathing, as you well know, is an involuntary action. We do it twenty-four hours a day, seven days a week without even thinking about it. Unless you've had an asthma attack, you may not know what it's like to gasp for air. In other words, it's a process you take for granted. Breath, in a real way, is the gift of life.

Through meditation, you increase your awareness of this involuntary action. You can turn your concentration toward this to focus on the inhaling, exhaling, rising, and falling off every breath. It becomes, in essence, the perfect object of mindfulness when you are beginning.

Chapter 11: Link Between Meditation And Stress/Depression, Anxiety And Happiness

Recently, researchers have connected fears of, and resistance to positive emotions to self-criticism. Self-criticism arises from past failures and the fear and uncertainty of the future. What you did wrong, whom you messed up with, what you failed to achieve, an opportunity that eloped you, where to get the money to pay all your bills, how your kids will grow up and when you will get a good job are some examples of our fears.

Our mind is so preoccupied with regrets about the past and fears about the future to an extent that we often find ourselves never even experiencing the goodness that is in the present. Meditation aims at taming the endless thoughts to help keep you grounded on the present (especially mindfulness meditation) since this ultimately helps you to enjoy the present as it unfolds.

Meditation involves our present moment while stress, depression, and anxiety are brought by our past and future. This is mostly the negative thoughts of our past failures. In many instances, when you remember about your past failure, you find yourself stressed. You can overcome this through constant meditation where you just feel your present moment.

In meditation, you just concentrate on something that is present. For instance, you focus on how you are breathing, your fingers, sound or just the quietness of the environment. This will leave your mind relaxed and therefore you will be happy. Additionally, through meditation techniques that we will learn in the next chapter, you start calming your breath, which in turn helps stabilize your blood pressure. This can in turn enable you to keep off anxious thoughts that can make it hard for you to be happy.

The result of being happy shows the connection between happiness and meditation. In short, you either meditate and become happy or fail to meditate and you start wallowing about the past and worrying about the future. These memories and thoughts will leave you stressed up and full of anxiety.

Chapter 12: Reflection To Soothe Anxiety

Also the clinical neighborhood will certainly confess that reflection benefits tension. While the majority of physician will certainly discount the suggestion of any kind of kind of different recovery approach, reflection is one that a lot of them could see advantages. It absolutely could not trigger any type of injury as well as has really been confirmed to aid you loosen up.

Among the key objectives for which reflection is utilized today in the West is to alleviate anxiety. As Americans end up being a lot more anxious out all the moment, they look for means to accomplish alleviation. Many individuals are searching for something to assist them as opposed to taking supplements or liquor.

Anxiety is the largest clinical dilemma that we deal with today. With many individuals searching for a remedy to ease themselves of anxiety, medical professionals are giving away depressants like they were sweet. Individuals proceed to be emphasized.

Proceeded anxiety plays mayhem on your main peripheral nervous system in addition to your body immune system. It could decrease your body immune system to ensure that all illness are practically welcomed right into your physical body. Why tinker anxiety when you can make use of reflection to aid you?

Reflection could soothe tension. It does labor, however it takes method. In order to make use of reflection to ease tension and also anxiousness, do the following:

Arrange a time to practice meditation each as well as every day. It will certainly be worth it in the lengthy run as the reflection begins to labor. As soon as you discover the reflection in fact laboring, it is like a light going on in a dark space.

Discover a peaceful location where you could rest as well as unwind that is tranquil. When you obtain utilized to practicing meditation, you will certainly be able to do this anywhere, also at your workplace workdesk.

If you are experiencing from anxiety or anxiousness, you could be attracted to take depressants or also a beverage. Reflection could soothe anxiety as well as anxiousness.

There are a selection of various reasons individuals deal with anxiety. The globe today is not the globe of HALF A CENTURY ago where points relocated at a much slower speed. Every little thing scoots as well as a lot of us attack off greater than we could eat in the endlessing look for obtaining "the globe and also every little thing in it.".

Reflection takes method. Does it labor to unwind you? It's been laboring for 5,000 years to loosen up individuals so opportunities are that it will certainly function on you.

This is why so several individuals make use of a concept when practicing meditation. Clearing up your head takes method, however when you are able to accomplish this, the globe of reflection is really open to you.

You could discover that you like to practice meditation over seeing tv and also desire to proceed with this technique. You might additionally locate that you want to find out even more concerning this old fine art and also start examining the technique of reflection via the ages as well as attempt to accomplish knowledge or an objective in life.

Scent could additionally be integrated with reflection. You could additionally make use of calming songs throughout your reflection technique.

If you could rest cross legged on the ground, penalty. Make certain that you are resting up so that you do not drop asleep. You desire to remove your head, not drop asleep.

Also clinical physicians will certainly recognize that reflection, particularly when integrated with breathing strategies, benefits you and also could soothe anxiety. There are signs that it reduces the high blood pressure along with increases the body immune system. The breathing workouts promote oxygen to your human brain as well as removing your head permits the invasive ideas that pester and also stress you to be done away with.

One of the points that emphasizes individuals out is invasive ideas. This is exactly what creates psychological tension. In order for reflection to be efficient, you have to remove your head of these invasive ideas.

Each time an invasive idea comes right into your mind, allow it go. Proceed to do this up until the things has your overall focus.

Tension could be a forerunner to a selection of various health problems, also cancer cells. The remedies for tension could be also a lot more damaging to your wellness compared to the anxiety itself. Depressants, which are usually recommended for tension, are extremely addicting and also have major side impacts.

While you are exercising this kind of overall focus, additionally technique breathing strategies. Take a deep breath in via your mouth, hold it for 5 secs and also after that take a breath out with your nose.

One of the main functions for which reflection is utilized today in the West is to alleviate tension. In order to utilize reflection to alleviate tension and also anxiousness, do the following:

Also clinical physicians will certainly recognize that reflection, specifically when incorporated with breathing strategies, is great for you as well as could alleviate tension. The treatments for anxiety could be also much more destructive to your health and wellness compared to the tension itself. Reflection could ease anxiety and also anxiousness.

Chapter 13: Meditation While Waiting

Waiting in line at the bank or for your appointment at the doctor's or dentist's provides you with a valuable opportunity to add meditation to your busy schedule. Since you are not doing anything for a few minutes, you can perform short guided mindfulness meditations so that you can put this otherwise wasted time to good use. Here are some exercises you can try.

Mindful Breathing

This is a very simple mindfulness meditation exercise that is very easy to learn, and it can be done either standing or sitting. All you have to do is simply to focus on the process of your breathing. Start by breathing in and out slowly; each cycle should take a few seconds. Inhale through your nose, feel the air move down your throat and into your lungs and then exhale through your mouth. You should feel the air flow freely during the breathing process with no difficulty.

While you're performing this exercise, keep your thoughts focused on your breathing. Clear your mind and focus on the physical sensations you are feeling as you breathe. You can do this exercise for a minute or two as a way to relax and calm yourself while you're waiting, and then work your way up to five minutes or longer.

Mindful Watching

This is another basic exercise that is easy to learn and may be more appropriate for you if you are more visually-oriented. You start this exercise by choosing an object in your immediate environment. It can be a picture that is hanging on the wall, or the table that is in front of you.

Once you've chosen your object, simply focus your attention on it. For example, let's say you choose to focus on the table in front of you. What color is it? What does the surface look like? How does the light hit it? Does it have imperfections? Look at it from every aspect. If it helps, you can imagine that you are looking at this object for the first time. Alternately, you can tell yourself that you will be asked to describe this object later. Allow yourself to be immersed in every detail of it visually.

Mindful Listening

This mindfulness exercise is similar to mindful watching, but focuses instead on the sense of hearing. You can do this either with eyes closed or open, depending on what you feel more comfortable with. Start the exercise by inhaling and exhaling slowly until you feel calm and ready to meditate.

Focus on what you hear around you. For example, you can focus on a sound that you hear in the distance, trying to hear it more distinctly. Alternately, if you have an mp3 player with you, you can also do this meditation with music. You can choose an old song that you have started to take for granted and then act as if you are listening to it for the first time. Listen to the way the different components of the record, such as the music and the vocals, work together.

The basic idea behind this meditation practice is to immerse yourself in the music without thinking about it. Don't have any judgmental thoughts about the music, simply focus on it for what it is. Simply listen to it as a piece of music.

Immersion

This is a more advanced meditation practice that you can try once you have mastered the simpler ones described previously. All you have to do is calm your thoughts and immerse yourself in your immediate environment. For this exercise, you will use several senses.

Start this exercise by slow breathing and centering yourself and then looking around you. Sit still and then immerse yourself in the environment surrounding you. Start by noting what you see, and then pay attention to what you hear. After that, you can start becoming mindful of the other senses. For example, what do you smell? What do you feel? Do you feel hot or cold? If it helps, you can imagine that you have to recreate the scene later and so try to notice as much about it as possible.

Gratitude

This is a meditation exercise that you can use to help develop positive feelings, particularly when you are feeling down. Simply think about something that you should be grateful for that you normally take for granted. For example, if you see sunlight coming in through the window, you can be grateful for the opportunity to be alive to see it. Or you can be grateful that you can appreciate its beauty.

Keep in mind that there are many people who cannot see the sunlight or are simply unable to be thankful for it. This is a good opportunity for you to look over the many small blessings in your life so that you can learn to recognize them and appreciate them.

Chapter 14: Create A Meditation Sanctuary

When you start meditating, you need to have a good meditation place. Of course anywhere could work. You don't need a fancy room or sacred spot or some kind of temple to begin your meditation. But your meditation sanctuary does need to meet a few requirements:

1.   It needs to be somewhere you feel safe. You can't enter the meditative state and let go of everything if you feel uneasy. A park may be nice, but if the random strangers and dogs wandering around make you uncomfortable, this isn't a good option. If you can't ever feel at ease at work, then don't meditate at work.

2.   It needs to be quiet. Lots of distractions will simply slip into your mind and mess up your meditation. Even if you

think that you can tune out voices and TV, you really can't. The brain is not good at tuning things out, as much as we like to think that it is. Instead of trying to strain out extra stimulus, simply create an area where you can be at peace.

3. It needs to be visually pleasing. This doesn't mean that your spot has to be perfect. But if the walls are painted a glaringly ugly yellow that repulses you, then you won't be able to enter the positive and peaceful energy state that you need to let go of stress. Make sure that your meditation sanctuary is visually appealing enough that it won't interfere with your meditation.

4. It needs to be a comfortable temperature. Room temperature is best, but everyone is different. Some people feel more at ease in slightly cool or even cold environments, while others like warmth. If the room you use is stuffy and

sweltering or unbearably cold for you, then you will be distracted and you won't feel comfortable. Find a good temperature where you can relax without worrying about shivering or sweating too much.

5.   It needs to be yours. This doesn't mean that you need to own the space. It could be a public area. But for the moment, it needs to be yours. No one can join you in this space while you meditate, unless you have a group or meditation buddy. If you are using a room in your house or workplace, lock the door and make sure that everyone understands not to disturb you until you come out.

Ideally, you are able to find a space that matches the above criteria. If you can't, then make do with what you can. Your car or your bedroom as you drift to sleep can work if need be. Just as long as a place is comfortable to you, it will work as a meditation sanctuary.

What to Put in Your Space

When you create your meditation space, consider it a little oasis from the rest of the world. The rest of the world may not intrude. This means that while you are meditating in this space, your phone, computer, TV, and other devices that connect you to the outside world must be off, or at least on silent so that they don't distract you.

Other people also can bring in disturbances. They may try to talk to you, or their coughing, sneezing, shifting, and other movements can continually pull you out of meditation. As you get better at meditating, you will eventually be able to meditate anywhere and block out distractions. But for now, you should avoid having people in your sanctuary while you meditate. If people are present, they should have the same goal as you, to relax and release tension, so they will behave in ways conducive and appropriate to meditation.

When it comes to what you should put in your sanctuary, a pillow or blanket is often a good idea. You can use a chair as well. Yoga mats can also suffice. Just bring in something that you can comfortably sit on. A hard floor or prickly carpet can create disturbances that disrupt your meditation. If you are using your bed, work on maintaining wakefulness. Falling asleep defeats the purpose of the meditation, but it is easy to slip into slumber when you are so completely relaxed.

Decorations don't need to be extravagant. You don't need to create a hippie den with lava lamps, bead curtains, harps, and patchouli dispensers. But this is your sanctuary, so add things that make you feel at home. If you are allowed to decorate this space, consider painting the walls a soothing shade of green or blue that will relax you. Add any decorations that soothe you without distracting you. Glaring pictures or graphics could provide distractions.

Try to rid the room of all electronics. TVs and computers definitely don't belong here. Even when off, they produce a hum and an energy field which can keep your nerves on edge. Other appliances, like refrigerators, also produce a constant faint electronic hum which can prevent your total relaxation, even if you don't consciously notice it. If you have no choice and can't reasonably remove electronics from your sanctuary, then at least turn them off and unplug them to halt the hum.

Replace harsh fluorescent lights with more relaxing options, such as candles or LED Christmas lights. I highly recommend getting a Himalayan salt crystal lamp. These lamps release negative sodium ions into the air which have been shown to have a calming effect on people. The light that they produce is also quite soothing and pretty. These lamps are always a conversation piece, as well.

Some people find crystals affect their vibrational energy. If you find that this is true, you can certainly add crystals to your sanctuary, or bring them and set them up around you if you are using a space that is not yours. Amethysts and emeralds are my preferred meditation stones.

The way the sanctuary smells is also important for relaxation. Some people like to burn incense while they meditate. Others like to use essential oils. I love essential oils because they are discreet. You don't have to fill a whole room that isn't yours with the smell of incense, you just dab a little essential oil on a napkin or scarf or your wrists and inhale it. Choose an essential oil that is designed to relax you and provide you with stress relief.

Incorporate it into your meditation by inhaling both before and after your practice.

Music can be soothing for some and distracting for others. You can experiment with silence and music in the background. Meditation music is often designed to both soothe your nerves and guide you along the mental journey of your particular meditation. You can find great musical tracks for free on Youtube or other sites online. Any music that is soothing to you will work, however. I once knew a guy who liked to meditate to metal. While most people would not find metal relaxing, he did and he was able to meditate more completely with it blasting in headphones. Just find what soothes you, regardless of what other people prefer, and use it to help you slide into relaxation.

Remember, this is all about you. This is your space and your time. So make it yours. Do what feels best to you. Don't let others tell you how to meditate. I am only providing you this advice to help you create a relaxing environment where your nerves are not being stimulated, but you can disregard any of these tips that don't work for you. Feel free to experiment and do what you think is right for you. If something doesn't work and seems to be preventing you from sliding into deep relaxation, then feel free to change it.

Make Everywhere a Sanctuary

Your sanctuary doesn't have to be the only relaxing place in your life, either. You should strive to make every place that you spend time in as relaxing as possible. People often make the mistake of thinking that relaxing lighting, colors, and other elements will make them sleepy and they choose to decorate with very stimulating items and colors. But lots of visual and auditory stimulus actually has the opposite effect on most people. Having a bright red or yellow room might make you feel energized at first, but quickly it will start to wear down on your energy levels and make you feel sleepy because it overwhelms your senses. Adding relaxing décor and colors will actually give you energy as your nerves calm down and you handle stress better.

Over time, work on making your entire home a sanctuary. You may not use your entire home for meditation, but having a relaxing home environment will make you feel so much better. You don't need to come home from a long day and be met by a messy, disorganized, loud, and stimulating home. That will just make you feel more exhausted and unhappy. And you won't know why.

Your bedroom in particular needs to become a place of rest. Cool or medium-spectrum colors and minimal décor is a good idea. Try to limit how many electronics you have in your bedroom. Also limit the activities that you engage in your room. Scientists say that for optimal sleep, you should use your bed for only sex and sleep. Eating, working, and doing other stimulating activities in bed can make your brain associate your bed with being awake. This will make sleep more difficult, which will throw your whole day and your ability to process stress way out of whack.

You may not have much control over how your workplace looks, but try to add little improvements where you can. Decorate your office or cubicle with relaxing pictures, use a salt lamp instead of fluorescents if you can, and try to minimize noise, multi-tasking, and distractions. If you have a window office, the outside view can be distracting, so keep the window covered. Keep the thermostat on as a comfortable a level as possible. Researchers are beginning to find that fluorescent lights and too-warm offices contribute to lots of sickness in employees, a phenomena known as sick building syndrome. Everyone will feel better and have more energy if they work in a more comfortable environment, with proper ventilation and a comfortable room-temperature thermostat setting.

It is OK to use essential oils throughout work. They won't put you to sleep. Also, give that coffeemaker a rest, as well as the candy dish. Instead, drink green tea. It has a little bit of caffeine and can really put you at ease. Again, it won't put you to sleep. For snacks, avoid heavy starches and eat an apple, banana, or celery sticks with cheese or peanut butter instead.

These snacks will help you keep off weight and they will provide you with more sustained energy over the course of the day. None of these things will relax you too much, despite the common phobia of allowing relaxation into the workplace. If anything, you will find that these things give you far more energy.

It may be hard to turn your entire home or office into a sanctuary. But you should try to treat everywhere that you go as a sort of sanctuary. While you are there, you need to feel good. Cut out the things that make you feel bad. Create as relaxing of an environment as you can. Americans are all under tremendous stress and we all need more serenity and order in our lives. Treating our living and work space like sanctuaries of peace, calm, and gentle conflict resolution and problem solving rather than drama can help us catch a brief break in the midst of our hectic lives.

Chapter 15: Different Types Of Meditation

You have probably heard of the benefits of meditation. But did you know there are several different types of meditation?

This chapter focuses on 5 different types of meditation and their ways to help your mind and body. Since the last couple of decades, the use of meditation significantly increased owing to the fact that people live more stressful lives and feel constant pressure, which results in increasing stress levels, which also produce many diseases.

Concentration method

This is the mother of all meditation techniques because concentrating on nothingness is the heart of meditation process. You need to train your mind to focus on an object, which is not an easy process and it takes time. On the start of your meditation journey, you are probably going to get distracted by all the problems you have but as the time passes, you will be getting better at what you do.

Reflective meditation

This is probably my favorite one as it involves concentrating on resolving a simple question for a certain period. In order to get good at reflective meditation, you first need to pass and master concentration method, which will take some time. The key in reflective meditation is to focus on resolving a specific question you asked yourself. If your mind tries to go on to another question, topic or a problem, you need to bring it back to the specific question.

Questions I recommend: Who am I? What is my purpose in life? What is my role in the universe? How can I make this world a better place?

Mindfulness meditation

This is one of the most powerful methods because it involves pain relief and it helps the most to those who are suffering from anxiety and depression.

However, this technique is not simple because it involves attention toward any action or object around you.

Creative meditation (visualization)

This one is very different because it is based on strengthening certain parts of your mind and emphasizing your qualities such as joy, compassion, humility, patience and many others. Or of you like you can describe this one as simply fantasizing and thinking of a fantasy version of your day or your future.

Chapter 16: Let's Get Started.

For your first experience with meditation you can follow these guidelines in order to start today. We will use a mindfulness type format since it's the most basic and common form practiced. A couple things important to note are: don't have unreasonable expectations (some would say to have no expectations), don't consume any caffeinated beverages or eat any food right before meditation, and take it easy!

To begin you should find a special place that you can do it every day and a comfortable posture to sit in. The reason it's good to find a specific place to do it every day is because this area will become associated with meditation in your mind making it easier to enter stillness. Some prefer to sit cross-legged while others prefer to sit on a straight backed chair. Either way is fine, but the key in posture is to ensure that your spine is straight and in a natural position. If you decide to sit cross-legged then you should place something under your buttocks such as a pillow in order to elevate your back end more. The purpose of this is to help your spine stay straight and relaxed. If your deciding to sit in a chair, then place your feet flat on the floor and try to keep yourself from using the chairs back as support. You want to be able to support yourself.

Once you're seated comfortably you may want to place your hands on your lap. It's not important how they are placed as long as it's comfortable for you. Next, tilt your head slight down towards your chest in to relax your neck. Doing this also helps to prevent mental excitement. You can choose to either close your eyes completely or leave them slightly open, whichever is most comfortable. Once you've done all of this, mentally observe each part of your body for signs of tension. Once you recognize an area in your body holding tension, allow yourself to let it go. You want to become relaxed, but also mentally aware.

Now that you're feeling comfortable and aware, turn your attention to your breathing. Observe how each breath goes in and out. Try to be aware of the physical sensations inside of your lungs as they expand and contract. Whenever your mind begins to veer off into thought land just simply observe the thought, let it pass, and return back to focusing on your breath. If this seems too overwhelming at first, then try counting your breaths. Start at one with your first outbreath and count up to thirty-three with each following outbreath. Once you reach thirty-three then count back down until you get to one. If you find yourself wandering off or you forget which number that you are on, then simply start over. If you still have more time left after doing this, then just try sitting in silence and focus on your breathing. The mental chatter should be much less after the counting. Do this for five minutes a day in the beginning and after two weeks try going up to ten minutes a day. This is literally it.

When you first begin your practice this mental chatter will seem very overwhelming, but don't get discouraged, this is normal. After a few weeks you will notice a significant drop in mental chatter and be able to access the stillness quite easily. The most important things when beginning a new practice is to maintain a routine. Tell yourself that you're going to do it every day at a specific time and do it, no matter what. If you do forget a day don't be hard on yourself, just continue when you remember and try harder to remember next time. It won't take long before this becomes an ingrained habit and it'll become second nature to remember to do it.

You can also practice meditation during regular everyday activities simply by being present. In order to accomplish this, you need only to observe whatever it is that you're doing with full focus. If you're washing your hands, then pay attention to the sound of the water as it comes out of the faucet and the way it feels on your hands. When you're walking somewhere pay attention to each step you take and your surroundings. This doesn't replace the practice of stillness, but it does help to increase your minds ability to focus.

Chapter 17: Christian Meditation

Meditation is usually done in order to get more enlightenment and also to transcend the mind in the Eastern traditions such as Daoism, Hinduism and so on. In the Christian way of meditating however, the purpose is to get purified or cleansed morally and to also gain a deeper understanding with the word of God or in the mystic way of Christian tradition, a greater closeness with God or Christ. There are various types of Christian meditative practices also and some of these practices will be discussed below.

Contemplative reading- Also known as contemplation, this practice requires the practitioner to deeply think about the happenings and teachings which are recorded in the bible.

Contemplative prayer- Most times, this entails a repetition of some certain sentences or words that are holy in a silent manner with total devotion and focus.

"Sitting with God"- This kind of silent meditation is usually done after contemplating or reading. The mind, soul and heart of the practitioner should be solely placed on God's presence.

Chapter 18: How To Prepare For Meditation?

So, you are convinced of the benefits of meditation, and you have finally made up your mind to meditate. What's next? How should you prepare for meditation for best results?

We would recommend you to prepare for meditation beforehand just like you would prepare for other activities – simply by thinking about it and planning well in advance.

Here are a few points which would keep you sorted:

•Fire up your motivation

Once you have found a secluded and isolated place where you can practice meditation single-mindedly, it is important to fire up your motivation. Ask yourself as to why you have chosen to meditate.

You might want to detoxify your mind, or to improve your mental skills or to achieve awakening – whatever your reason is, it is necessary to think of your main inspiration to be able to meditate better.

You do not have to judge your reasons or label them as small or big. All that is needed is the right acknowledgement of these reasons. Once you feel motivated, you would be better able to deal with the negative thoughts and resistance that your body might through while meditating.

•Set realistic goals

Goals are important for every task, and it is necessary that they are reasonable enough so that you are not disappointed in the end. It is highly recommended to set goals and keep a tab on your expectations in this particular session.

Some of these goals could be staying alert and not feeling drowsy or controlling your thought process, or being able to meditate for an hour or two. Whatever your goals are – make sure that you know them beforehand so that you can work in the right direction to achieve them.

•Beware of expectations

Settings goals and working in the right direction to achieve them is important. But it is equally important to be aware of your ambitious expectations. This would make way for disappointment.

For instance, you might want to control your mind from wandering a certain day. But if this doesn't happen, do not disappoint. Disappointment would make the entire practice tough and you would gradually even lose your interest.

It is highly recommended to work in the right direction to achieve your daily set goals, but in an event when you are not able to achieve them, do not let this disappointment weigh you down.

It is important to understand and accept the fact that you would not progress every single day. There will be plateaus when nothing would change for days, and it is normal. Thus, stay relaxed and keep working in the right direction to achieve your goals.

Always remember that meditation always benefits you, and there is no such thing as 'bad meditation.'

•Meditate diligently

Meditating diligently means engaging in the process whole-heartedly instead of simply daydreaming. It is natural to feel tempted towards more exciting and entertaining things like a night out with your friends, or a movie marathon.

But do not let these toxic thoughts from diverting your schedule. Always remember that it is a trap. If you skip your meditation schedule for a single day, it will soon become a practice and you will find it hard to get back on track.

The best way to deal with this is to keep continuing the practice whenever you are in doubt. Convince yourself that you are not going to skip meditation and other important things can wait when you are done with your session for the day.

•Review potential distractions

To be able to perform meditation in the best way, it is highly recommended to keep your mind free from any possible distractions. Thus, before sitting for meditation, it is highly recommended to drink enough water so that you don't feel thirsty.

Additionally, perform a quick review of things which you think would fall in your way. For instance, a heated argument at your workplace or regrets about the past or money issues and the like.

Acknowledge these issues beforehand and try to avoid thinking about them if they distract you while meditating. You might not be successful about the first attempt, but just setting the intention will make things pretty easier.

•Check your posture

Before you start meditating, it is highly recommended that you adopt a proper posture and feel comfortable. Here is a quick checklist of all the things that you need to have a look at:

• Sit comfortably and adjust your supports

- Align your head, back and neck properly and make sure that you are neither leaning forward and nor backwards and nor to the sides.

- Your muscles should be balanced, shoulders even and hands should be at the same level.

- Your lips should be closed and your tongue should rest against the roof of the mouth.

- Close your eyes and position yourself slightly downward as if you are reading something. This would create the least tension in your face and forehead.

- Next, breathe naturally without controlling or forcing it.

- Soak yourself in the process and enjoy. Release any tension and just focus on the now. Keep thoughts to the minimum.

Chapter 19: Understanding & Nurturing Mindfulness

It is important that you understand that you attitude to life makes all of the difference and you should use this attitude to develop your capacity to be mindful, in order to live a greater mindful life. The key attitudes to nurture mindfulness are as follows:

-       Curiosity – become curious about your experience. How are your emotions? What thoughts are you having? How would you describe how your body currently feels?

-       Acceptance – this does not mean resignation, mindfulness is accepting how you feel now rather than denying it, acceptance comes first, and change will come later.

-        Kindness – bring warm, caring compassion to the moment, and experience this moment with your heart and your head.

-       Letting Go – there is no need to hold onto pleasant experiences or push away unpleasant ones, let go and don't dwell on what has gone.

-        Non – judging – see what you experience as it is rather than classifying it as good, bad or indifference.

- Non – striving – experience whatever it is as it is rather than creating a goal and striving to attain different experiences.

- Patience – be patient as change takes time.

- Trust – let your inner self guide you and have confidence in your mindfulness.

- Beginner's mind – look after yourself and grow as a beginner not trying to be an expert. The beginner's mind has many possibilities so use them.

The most powerful way to develop mindfulness is through mindfulness meditation. Probably the most popular form of mindfulness meditation is mindfulness of breath, which involves being mindfully aware of your breath.

Try following the steps below to try mindfulness meditation:

1. Be aware if the sense of your breath – there is no need to change the rate of your breath, simply feel the sensation of your breath entering and leaving your body.

Feel your breath in your nose, throat, chest and down in your stomach, where possible you should focus on the breath in your stomach as this will make you feel more relaxed.

2. When your mind wanders, bring it back – it is natural for your thoughts to stray from what you want to focus on, do not worry as soon as you become aware that you have drifted gently bring your mind

back to your breath if this is what you are focusing on.

Mindfulness is really as simple as that. Try to bring a sense of mindfulness attitude to your experiences such as kindness, acceptance and curiosity and so forth. This exercise can be practiced for just a minute or as long as an hour, it really depends on you.

Understanding the Aspects of Mindfulness

Mindfulness engages three processes which come together to bring about the state of awareness.

-	Intention – This is what you hope to get from practicing mindfulness, you could be looking for stress reduction, greater emotional balance to truly discover you. The strength of your intention is what motivates you to practice mindfulness daily and it is what makes the quality of your mindful awareness.

-        Attention – Mindfulness is about paying attention to both inner and outer experiences, with your mindful attention being developed through a variety of meditation.

-      Attitude – Mindfulness see you having to pay attention to certain attitudes like kindness, acceptance and curiosity.

Using Mindfulness as a coping mechanism for difficult emotions

Everyone has bad days, some worse than others, however when emotions get the

better of us we can use the RAIN formula
to manage feelings in a mindfulness way.

R – Recognize what you are feeling; name
the emotion in your mind if you can

A – Accept the experience that you are
going through, you probably won't like the
feeling

I – Investigate – become curious about the
experience, which part of your body is
feeling it and what are you thinking

N – Non – Identification – View the
experience as an even that will pass, after
all different emotions come and go within
you but they are not you

Chapter 20: Simple Lifestyle Changes To Reduce Stress

A healthy lifestyle is a significant compliment to any stress relief program. You can enhance your stress resistance and general health by avoiding tobacco, caffeine and excessive alcohol, eating a diet rich in a wide range of whole grains, fruits, and vegetables, and getting regular exercise. Here are some other tips:

Maintain an organized living space

Living in a cluttered environment can drain your energy and lead to additional stress. On the other hand, a soothing and beautifully decorated environment can be a haven for escaping your life stressors. Some of the ways you can work towards creating a beautiful and orderly living space is to declutter your home, get organized about cleaning, or even practice Feng Shui.

Learn to schedule your time

When you keep a schedule, learn to say no to additional demands on your time, and take advantage of shortcuts in your life, you will become less frantic, and more available to do the things you really love and enjoy in your life.

Establish a supportive social circle

People who have a supportive social circle, or simply one close partner or friend to talk to and rely on in times of crisis are able to live healthier and less stressful lives. If you commit yourself to better develop your current relationships and meet more people, you will find that the benefits are well worth the trouble.

Take care of your body

You are better equipped to deal with the stressors in your life when your body is healthy and in a good condition. But an unhealthy body can result in tremendous amounts of additional stress. Some of the ways you can take care of your body include getting enough sleep, exercising regularly, eating a healthy diet, pampering yourself, and getting massages.

Renew your spirit

People tend to carry stress in their bodies, and keep it in their minds. As such, a stressful experience can stay with you and keep affecting you long after the real experience has ended. Stress management in your daily life can be much easier on your emotional, physical and mental state when you take regular breaks from your stress.

Chapter 21: Urge Surfing Meditation

That are not always good for him. For example, even if someone is on a diet, he may feel the urge to eat junk foods, or to eat a lot of carbs, even if he's not supposed to. People are susceptible to temptation.

A person's urges could be likened to a wave. Sometimes, that wave surges and it overwhelms you; it surrounds you. According to the late, great psychologist Alan Marlatt, PhD, people often have the urge to switch back to their old habits, no matter how negative those may seem to be. Just like waves, urges also rise in intensity, and you get to feel them enveloping you. And just like waves, you can also surf on your urges and emerge victorious.

But, remember, your urges are not who you are, and you still have so much control over them. There are basically 4 stages to surfing those urges, and these are:

1.   Acknowledge the urge—and how you experience it.

2.   Focus on a certain part of your body where you feel like you experience the craving the most.

3.   Take a deep breath, and release tension as you do so.

4.   Repeat the focus on the part of your body that sees the craving.

According to Dr. Sarah Bowen of the Center for the Study of Health and Risk Behaviors at the University of Washington, every person has the capacity to fight his urges in ways that he knows best. People cope via experience, and that's why they have to strengthen their minds so it would be easier to control urges and other things in life.

Urges peak for around 20 to 30 minutes and in that span of time, you can shut them down, too! Take a look at the techniques below to find out how you could say goodbye to your urges!

Urge Surfing could be done whenever you feel like your urges are taking over your mind. This way, you can stop yourself from going back to your old habits—and you can stop new bad habits from forming, too!

Urge Surfing Exercises

1. Close your eyes and try to understand where in your body do you experience the urges. Just sit somewhere quiet, remember an urge, and then shift attention to where you feel the said urge in your body. Take note that this differs from person to person so you really

cannot compare it with them. Just try to find a situation that feels closest to you, and focus on that.

2. Try to picture the said situation as specific as you can in your mind, and then turn your attention back into it.

3. Once you have focused your attention there, get lost in the moment and notice the sensations that you feel. Is there any saturation? Do you feel some kind of tingling sensation there? Do you see or feel or sense colors in any way? Be objective and not judgmental. Just because you have recognized something does not mean you have to judge yourself for it.

4. Draw an imaginary outline around the place where you felt the sensation and notice how you feel after doing so.

5. Focus on your breathing, and watch it change in a matter of 1 to 2 minutes.

Even if you feel like your breathing patterns have not changed, do not skip this part. You may also try saying the words "breathe in", and "breathe out", if you think that would make it easier for you to focus.

6.   After doing that breathing exercise, focus on the part where you felt the urges again.

7.   Again, notice how those parts of your body feel, or if there are certain sensations that you currently feel there. You can breathe in and out again if you feel like it will help, and then watch the sensations change. Try to do this for at least a minute—or longer, if you still could.

8.   Now, imagine that your urges are waves, and the sensations you feel are also what you feel while facing a real wave. Try to imagine the wave rising and

falling as the sensations inside you reach their peak and then subside.

9.   Now, try to use your breath as a means to ride the said waves, and just pretend that you are a pro-surfer and that the wave will not be able to consume you. Try thinking of this for a minute or so; again, the longer, the better.

10.   Ride the said wave and think of the sensations in an objective, non-judgmental way. You'd probably feel some warmth in your belly as the sensations increase.

11.   Then, after surfing the urge, go ahead and congratulate yourself. Remind yourself that you actually could kick those urges away—especially if you want to!

It's best to practice this every day, or on a regular basis. This way, it would be easier for you to trump your urges down!

Chapter 22: How To Remove Stress

Do you know what stress actually is?

It's a reaction of your body to the experiences you have throughout a day or even a life. We identify stress as extremely negative thing because it interrupts our immune system and our life. But, there is also one different way of looking at stress. Stress can be a guiding tool.

If you watch a movie and you don't like the actors or it's too violent, you switch the program, right?

The same thing you can do with stress.

Your body shows you in many ways the real condition you are in (sweating, insomnia, crazy heartbeats, indigestion, depression, despondency). So, stress and indicators of stress can really save us by telling us to go away and switch to another program.

Can it really be that easy? Let's see.

Do you feel stuck at your work and you hate every morning of your week when you wake up? Quit your job. You only live once and there are tons of jobs out there. No apology for that.

Is your partner not treating you well? Are you in a miserable relationship? Just say goodbye and switch to something better. Why waste your precious time? Yes, it's that easy.

Do you think that everybody relies on you and you never tell anyone no? It's time to say no and be your own best friend.

Do you have a blurred vision of your life but you are also confused, insecure, and full of fear for the future, and it all makes you feel so stressed? Set some goals and work every day, day by day to reach them.

Find time to relax. You will see the solution when you start doing things that are out of your comfort zone. Sometimes life can be so simple and beautiful, yet we people make it so complicated. It seems like we love that. No situation in life is irreparable. We just need to be awake and try to do our best.

It is important to learn that what matters more than the event that causes stress itself is usually our thoughts about the event when we are trying to manage stress. Again, meditation helps you stay calm in stressful situations.

How you see that stressful event will be the largest single factor that impacts your physical and also mental health.

Only your interpretation of events and challenges in life can be used to decide whether they are invigorating or harmful for you. So, you are the one that decides about your life and whether this"stressful thing"will affect you or not.

This is your life and your journey, I hope I helped you a little bit with this book to realize that power is in your hands and you can achieve anything you want, if you really want it.

"The best freedom is being yourself"

Chapter 23: Meditation "Visualization Of Emptiness In The Body."

The right hand is placed on the abdomen, just below the navel, left rests on top. Next, we need to straighten the back, slightly lower the jaw, tongue resting on the palate, eyes closed, looking internally to focus on the tip of the nose.

Let go of thoughts and try to visualize your body. Visualization occurs through visual images and inner feelings. As soon as you feel the contours of the body, use your imagination and imagine that it is empty. The emptiness will begin to expand as if you are entering a field of unfolding space in your consciousness. From head to toe, just visualize emptiness. If you find it difficult to visualize the emptiness of the whole body, try to imagine the emptiness in parts. Say you start with a visualization of the emptiness of your head, then neck, chest, and so gradually reaching the consciousness of the whole body. While having this feeling of the dissolution of the inside of the body, nonetheless keep your visualization of its contours. After that, all that is required in your field of awareness is to increase or decrease your body size from that of a mustard seed to the borders of the Universe.

The practice of visualizing the emptiness of the body requires a degree of perseverance and diligence until a very clear vision of the empty body is achieved.

The effect of:

-The student will be rewarded for their work by a state of ease, joy and clarity.

Chapter 24: How Does Meditation Affect Stress Levels?

Stress can logically be characterized as "battle or flight". Stress is fundamentally a physiological reaction invigorated by debilitating or unsavory circumstances. A disagreeable circumstance here can shift from individual to individual, it contrasts with discernment. Additionally, certain requesting circumstances can make stress, requests which one can't satisfy. There are a few methods for treating stress, some normal and others being simulated. Regular ways are the best favored and meditation is one of those common structures.

There can be a few wellsprings of stress - the tumults in human personality and the waves are for the most part in charge of stress. A mind isn't free; it is really our point of view. Once these considerations begin administering once again us, we are under stress. The human manner of thinking is a perpetual procedure, it proceeds forever. Again these musings are not extremely strong sources that could manage over us, it's simply that they overwhelm us on occasion with certain dubious techniques. We should attempt and break down these circumstances and be quiet. I know it intense, at that point you may need to look for enabling, you to can reflect, it helps a ton.

Meditation to stress resembles light to haziness, both can't exist together. General meditation helps in keeping the psyche and the body free from stress. Meditation is simply the most ideal method for healing from numerous such physiological issues. Meditation helps in keeping up a legitimate harmony between the psychological, enthusiastic and physical conditions of a human personality.

Meditation can't be characterized in like manner terms; it really fluctuates with the setting of utilization. All we know is that intervention is perhaps the best and the most powerful method for stress help. Everything began as a religious technique, a training utilized by religious individuals and Hinduism is the wellspring of its starting point.

Meditation is being utilized as a strategy for treatment now; it is additionally utilized with the end goal of hand to hand fighting, practice, and other wellbeing medicines. Medicinal enables your psyche to unwind and rest settled; it is genuinely a method for detaching yourself from the outer world. This material world and everything identified with it causes stress, attempt to take some time out from your day by day plan, it is for yourself I let you know and for your advantage also. Likewise, meditation encourages you to enhance mentally. It upgrades your psychological capacities, sharpness and overall prosperity.

Meditation performs at 3 levels, physical, mental and profound level. Each unsettling influence happening in these levels can be mended with the assistance of meditation. It causes you discharge stress, uneasiness, pressure and repulsive circumstances.

How can one think?

The sitting stance is vital while contemplating. Sit in a casual position with your eyes shut and mind cleared. Attempt to center around a specific sound or protest, take a full breath and proceed with this procedure for no less than 20 minutes.

Meditation helps in expanding the level of sympathy and persistence. It hones memory and improves your mindfulness.

A large portion of the stress reliefs have symptoms, however, meditation being one of the characteristic methods for discharging stress has no reactions by any means. Everything it does is clear your brain. Additionally, there are no types of gear or costs included.

Meditation is one of a kind strategy with characteristic healing forces.

Chapter 25: Meditation and Awareness

Meditation is like other activities you practice. Its benefits will spread into the rest of your life. For example, you might love to rock climb but work in an office. If you examine your job superficially—shuffling papers, typing on a computer, attending boring meetings—you might argue that rock climbing does nothing for you at work. However, if you dig a little deeper, you might notice that when you sit at your chair, your posture is strong and erect because the muscles in your back are in good shape. When you come into work in the morning, you might notice your coworkers drinking coffee or energy drinks to counteract their sleepiness. However, you know that the only way to be successful in a rock climb in the morning is to get lots of good, healthy sleep the night before. This attitude has you shutting off the Netflix in the evening and getting to bed early. This healthy approach to living is out of respect for a body that you're going to ask to free climb 1000 feet in the air next weekend.

Meditation has a similar effect on your everyday life. By learning to relax, you can calm your body during tense situations, reducing your heart rate and lowering your blood pressure. But meditation's biggest benefit is increased awareness. Because you have learned to focus your mind through meditation, you will find yourself more capable of focusing it on the tasks you have in front of you. When distractions attempt to derail your attempts to get your work done, you are abler to resist them—e.g. acknowledging an email that you must reply to but putting it aside until you have completed your report.

We will have more to learn about awareness later on, in particular about an inner awareness that is the goal of meditation itself. But for now, take stock of how meditation is affecting your everyday life and how it has a positive effect on many aspects of your day.

Chapter Summary. The benefits of awareness in your life due to meditation:

• Meditation has many positive effects on a person's everyday life.

• Awareness and the ability to focus on life's tasks get stronger the longer a person practices meditation.

Conclusion

A positive attitude teaches you that anything is possible. With positivity, you are confident and more willing to take on new challenges. You are ready to face the world and you will not be afraid to conquer your fears.

I encourage you to read this book again and use it as a reminder of how you can continue to implement a positive mindset. It is one of the greatest strategies that we as humans can develop and train ourselves to do.

It may not be easy to remain positive especially when tough situations arise, but remember that you have power over your emotions, and you are the only one who can control what you are doing, how you feel toward situations, and how you respond to others.

Continue to make positive thinking a daily practice until it becomes a habit, which — as stated previously — takes 30 days of conscious effort to form.

About The Author

JOSEPH TOLLE is born wth the vision to promote the art of meditation among the masses. The author has written several research papers on the topic. He has served as an instructor promoting various cultural arts in University of San Francisco. He is currently living with his wife in Toronto

CPSIA information can be obtained
at www.ICGtesting.com
Printed in the USA
BVHW090857151121
621685BV00016B/1016

9 781989 682654